Polo the Magnificent:
The Story Of The Dribbling Magician

Polo the Magnificent: The Story Of The Dribbling Magician

Nii Odai Anidaso Laryea

DAkpabli

DAKPABLI & ASSOCIATES
ACCRA

POLO THE MAGNIFICENT: THE STORY OF THE
DRIBBLING MAGICIAN

ISBN: 97899889022 7 8

Editor: Nana Awere Damoah

Book Layout by multiPIXEL Limited
P O Box DC 1965, Dansoman, Accra, Ghana
Email: jkojoyanney@gmail.com
Tel: +233 302 333 502 | +233 246 725 060 | +233 246 210 862

Published by
DAkpabli & Associates
P O Box 7465, Accra North, Accra, Ghana
Tel: +233 264 339 066 | +233 244 704 250 | +233 247 896 375
Email: info@dakpabli.com

Foreword

By Ken Bediako

I thought I was the undisputed number one admirer of the reputed Dribbling Magician Mohammed Ahmed Polo until I had the privilege of reading this narration by Nii Odai Laryea and I quickly had to revise my notes. Nii Odai Laryea is, in fact, fanatical about Polo to a fault. In his estimation Polo is the most colourful player to wear the football boots for money. The world is yet to see a more attractive footballer than the Nima-born football artiste. I doff my hat for Nii Odai Laryea.

I was Sports Editor of the mass circulation Daily Graphic in 1973 when Polo hit the limelight with his amazing football skills. I have to disclose the fact I was among the group of sports writers that gave Polo the appellation 'Dribbling Magician', later on progressing to 'Dribbling Professor' after many other accolades had been showered on him. The young boy was not only an amazing dribbler and fantastic passer of the ball, but he could score some vital goals especially when the going was becoming tough for his team. Mr. Emmanuel Amoako, my deputy at the sports desk, came up with the tag 'the scorer of important goals'.

I was so fond of the young dribbler who made the art of ball-juggling part of himself – like breathing – so much so that I decided in my capacity as the Sports Editor to cover majority of the matches he featured in. This practice continued for a long time and I used all the superlatives I could assemble. There were times I had to struggle to find new words to describe Polo's football artistry. I was short of vocabulary.

I recall the famous 'Miracle of El Wak' in 1977 when Hearts of Oak had to conjure three amazing goals in the second half to beat visiting Mufulira Wanderers of Zambia to erase a 5-2 defeat in an Africa Cup semi-final second leg. My excitement and desire to paint an exceptional vivid picture of Polo's contribution to Hearts success that day took me an unusually long time to finish writing the story. I had to change my introduction several times until my senior colleague, the late Yaw Boakye Ofori Atta, drew my attention to the fact that my fanaticism for Polo was delaying production, amidst laughter from my colleagues.

I admired Polo to the hilt and even initiated the formation of a 'Polo Fan Club' that existed only on paper, using the Sports columns of the Daily Graphic to continually celebrate his birthday; I was that fanatical but please wait until you finish reading Nii Odai Laryea's narration and you will find mine to be child's play.

Acknowledgement

Gratitude first goes to Almighty Jehovah God for bringing to completion what He helped me to start a few years ago, even though it had been a dream for years. To Him be the glory!

I am also very grateful to my family members who gave me the encouragement and stood by me through thick and thin – Dorcas (my Prime Minister), Afote Asempa, Niifio Adom and Mensah Sowaba (my three young men). To my cousin, Bro. Kaarl Laye, who broke the news about the arrival of the football gem to me, I doff my hat. He, together with other family relations and close friends like my brother T. T. Laryea Jnr., Edmund Osekre, Theophilus Martey Botchway, Prof. Philip Laryea, Abraham Laryea, Nicholas Tettey Kwashie Pardie, Bro. Harry Attafuah-Appiah and Edem Djokotoe, threw their weight behind me with unyielding support and gave me the requisite stimulus to operationalise the good intentions of yesteryear.

Some literary luminaries who have also been a great source of encouragement deserve special appreciation e.g. Ackah Anthony, Uncle Ebo Whyte, Prof. Kwabena Nsiah, Nana Awere Damoah, Flora Amerley Olleenu, Dan Dzide and Kwame Nyarko. Others include the late Sammy Okaitey (Graphic Sports), late Prof. Kwesi Andam (former Vice Chancellor of KNUST), Messrs. I. K. Edusei, Ken Bediako,

Magnus Rex Danquah and Maxwell Arthur.

Gratitude is extended to colleagues of the Soccer Professor especially 'Goal Thief' Peter Lamptey, 'Super' Sam Suppey, 'Thunder' Anas Seidu and Evans Aryeequaye who shared practical experiences about the rare qualities they found in Ahmed Polo.

Messrs. Maxwell Koranteng and T. V. Musah, former Hearts of Oak management staff members, encouraged me immensely and provided insights about their perspectives of the Dribbling Magician.

My boss, the indefatigable Mr. Mawuena Dotse (Prof), has always been a tower of strength and a great source of inspiration to me in my writing and I am eternally grateful to him.

To many others whose names time and space would not permit me to mention, I am grateful.

Dedication

The book is dedicated to my WARREDOC '90 mates who constituted our non-aligned movement (NAM) team in Colombella, Perugia, Italy. They made me enjoy playing football and writing about it.

The team (in which I was a midfielder) includes Dr. Issiaka Savane (Cote d'Ivoire, as goalkeeper with Josefino Capati from the Philippines as reserve goalie), full backs Dr. Apichai Thirathon (Thailand) and Senih Yazghan (Turkey), half backs Wilfred Oluwasegun Alegbeleye (Nigeria) and Danilo Hadjukovic (erstwhile Yugoslavia). Our midfield was made up of Hanny Hassan (Egypt, outside right), Ben Conteh (Sierra Leone, outside left) and Dennis Salgado (also known as 'Hard Rock', Ecuador). Our strikers were the late Emmanuel Nkrumah (a.k.a. Moving Average, Ghana) and Zoran Petreski (otherwise called Maradona, erstwhile Yugoslavia). Reserves include Sam Sanya Kabita (Uganda), Setargew Demiliew (Ethiopia) and Mohmmmed Taha (Sudan), team doctor Rolando Maileg (Philippines) and coaches Dr. Bernard Goue (Cote d'Ivoire), Placide Appalo (Benin) and Ing. Ms. Maria Claudia Benevidez Delgado (Colombia). Last but not the least were our tripartite hosts: Enrico, Michelle and Fabrizio Brensachi as well as Reina Isabella Perez Monteverde (Venezuela) and Mattiga Panumtharalnichagul (Thailand).

Contents

Chapter 1

Ghana's Soccer Stars

The Wonder Boy

Ghana, no doubt, is a great soccer nation; having churned out many talented footballers and stars since the game was introduced into the country decades ago. To date, three sets of stars appear to make Ghana's 'All-Time-Teams' (occasionally I had more than three for a position). These I got through interactions with a number of soccer personalities, sportswriters and fans countrywide. The players were selected based on their contribution to the national team, their respective clubs, general discipline and, occasionally, their influence on the international scene (for those who played professional soccer outside). I produce the sets below:

No	Team A	Team B	Team C
1	Robert Mensah	*Joseph Carr	*Richard Kingson
2	Frank Crentsil	*Dan Oppong	*Haruna Yusif
3	Oliver Acquah	*Ofei Ansah	*Akuetteh Armah (99 Styles)/ *Hesse Odamtten
4	Willie Evans	*Joe Addo	*Sammy Osei Kuffuor/ *Isaac Acquaye/ Awuley Quaye
5	Addo Odametey	John Eshun	*Kuuku Dadzie
6	Ibrahim Sunday	*Adolf Armah	Kwame Nti/ James Adjei
7	Osei Kofi	Baba Yara	*Albert Essuman/ *Yaw Sam
8	Wilberforce Mfum	Jones Attuquayefio	*Michael Essien/ C. K. Gyamfi
9	Edward Acquah	*Dan Owusu & *Kwasi Owusu	*Tony Yeboah/ *Asamoah Gyan
10	*Abdul Razak	*Abedi Ayew	Aggrey Fynn/ *Stephen Appiah, *Opoku Nti/ *Edwin Conduah
11	*Ahmed Polo	Mohammed Salisu	*Malik Jabir/ *Francis Kumi

*Players I watched myself; the others (without asterisks) were picked from interviews conducted among 120 fans I interviewed who watched the players in the 1960s and early 1970s.

One would realise that I have not mentioned equally great stars like goal keepers John Naawu, Addoquaye Laryea, John Baker, John Botchway, Edward and Salifu Ansah, Owusu Mensah, Dodoo Ankrah, Sannie Abdulai and Abukari Damba. Defenders like Frank Amankwaah, Kwasi Appiah, Seth Ampadu, Anthony Dwemoh, Sampson 'Gadaffi' Lamptey, Justice Moore, Dogo Moro, Michel Lomo, John Mensah, P.S.K. Paha and Isaac Paha and Tetteh Gorleku have not featured. Neither has space been found for schemers and strikers in the likes of Kofi Pare, John Nketiah Yawson, Joe Ghartey, Tetteh Chandu, Augustine Arhinful, Emmanuel Osei Kuffuor, Ishmael Addo (three times 'goal-king'), Karimu 'Star Boy', George 'Jair' Alhassan, Ben Kayede, Emmanuel Quarshie, Opoku Afriyie, Agyeman Prempeh, Joe Sam, Windsor Kofi Abbrey, Frank Odoi (VC 10), Kofi Badu, Sulley Muntari and many more. The list appears endless. This clearly indicates that Ghana abounds in soccer talent. The difficulty in naming Ghana's all-time best is that the players excelled at different points in our football history.

My personal best for Ghana's All-Time 11 has **Robert Mensah** in goal, full-backs **Dan Oppong** and **Akuetteh Armah (99 Styles),** half-backs **Seth Ampadu** and **Addo Odametey** with **Osei Kofi** on the right wing and **Ahmed Polo** on the left wing. While the midfield would be made up of **Ibrahim Sunday**, Joe Sam and **Abdul Razak,** the striker who would complete the squad would be Dan Owusu. My reserves would be **Joe Carr** as goalkeeper, **Haruna Yusif** and

Oliver Acquah as full backs, half-backs **John Eshun** and **Kuuku Dadzie,** with midfielders **Adolf Armah** and **Abedi Ayew 'Pele'.** Strikers would be **Wilberforce Mfum, Edward Acquah** and/or **Tony Yeboah. Can you imagine such a squad lining up at the World Cup stage?**

By and large, however, when many fans and soccer analysts are requested to name the brightest and biggest of this array, two names that often come to the fore include the **Wizard Dribbler** Reverend Osei Kofi and **Dribbling Magician** Alhaji Ahmed Polo. This book attempts to look at the latter since I was not privileged enough to watch Osei Kofi. The two soccer icons made a large and deep impact on the game in Ghana from the 1960s to the late 1990s. When the late 'Sir' Cecil Jones Attuquayefio was asked a few years ago to mention who he considered as Ghana's best footballer ever, he paused for some minutes and replied "…it will be difficult for me to settle on only one. I will go for two footballers – a right winger in the person of Osei Kofi and the other a left winger in the person of Ahmed Polo." Indeed just recently (11/11/2020) when Hearts of Oak Football Club celebrated its 109th anniversary, its long-term Board Secretary, Ernest Thompson, remarked that the all-time best players of the club are Addo Odametey and Mohammed Ahmed Polo (www.ghanaweb.com).

I have used more than ten (10) indicators that are often employed internationally in appraising a player's performance. Ahmed Polo has them all and passes these tests with distinction. These include issues such as natural talent, accuracy of passing, conversion of set pieces, temperament on the field of play, team-play and dribbling. Others include effective use of both feet, use of the head, pace, variation of style, effective game diagnosis, shots, stamina, contribution to club and country, loyalty etc. Hardly does one come by players who possess and combine more than five of these indicators or attributes very well and, yet, Polo possesses more than enough of them as depicted in the tale below. Over all, he scores over 90% and I wonder how many good players can attain scores more than 100 over 150. In my estimation and from my perspective, perhaps, only two players – the great Diego Armando Maradona and Pele (Edson Arantes do Nascimento) – would score more than 138/150.

Indicators	Maximum points	Polo's score
Loyalty and dedication	10	9.5
Contribution to club and country	10	9.5
Pace	10	9
Stamina	10	9.5
Shots	10	9
Variation of style	10	9.5
Dribbling	10	9.5
Effective use of both feet	10	8.5
Effective use of the head	10	8.5
Discipline (on and off the field)	10	9
Conversion (effective use) of set pieces	10	9.5
Accuracy of passing	10	9.5
Team-play	10	9.5
Tackling/ defensive play	10	8.5
Number of years of play & impact	10	9.5
Total	150	138

"I started watching football in Ghana from the 1970s. Two footballers who I find to be the best then are 'Golden Boy' Abdul Razak and 'Wonder Boy' Ahmed Polo but Polo was a shade better than Razak. Polo had all the qualities to make him Ghana's greatest. In spite of not scoring too many goals, he had a way of spraying defense-splitting passes that created chaos in the opponents area any time he wished, distributed flawlessly to colleagues up-front, provided the 'enabling environment' for strikers to score and thrilled fans with his exquisite dribbling skills...technically, I find him to be the best ever." – **Carl Tuffuoh, Sports Enthusiast & Commentator**

*Taken around 1973, this photograph of the Black Stars shows some of Ghana's best ever including some great players in the past. Front row (from right to left): 'Duru' Lante France, Akuetteh Armah (99 Styles), **Ahmed Polo (then about 16/17 years of age)**, Isaac Eshun… P. S. K. Paha, Sam Aryee Acquah, Abdul Razak, Sam Amarteifio and Kwasi Owusu. Standing (from right to left): Goalie Botchway, Mama Musah…Joe Ghartey, Joe Sam, Malik Jabir…Lomo Michelle, George Alhassan, Robert Hammond, Ibrahim Sunday & Brazilian coach Oswaldo Sampaio.*

Chapter 2

THE MAGNIFICENT!

As soon as he appeared

On Ghana's soccer landscape,

One could tell that this was the arrival

Of a special superstar;

He could soar into the skies and dance on the field,

He could weave and waltz his way

Through a thousand tackles

And dazzle the fans with his magic.

One time he is seen in defense

Collecting a pass,

Another time in midfield

Distributing with perfect precision,

Yet another time feigning a move

And feinting in different directions.

What a player!

He held the key

To the tightest of defenses,

Place many defenders on him,

He would evade them all

With flair and flamboyance,

He could curl the ball

With a delicate touch

Keeping it to that enigmatic left foot

As though with a magnet

Letting go at goal only

When all the tailor-measured passes

Failed to produce results from colleagues.

What a player!

How come Polo was only kept

In Ghana and Africa's envelope?

He shot to fame before the 1990s

When talented Black players were yet to really open

The doors to showcase their talents in Europe,

Injuries, the archenemy of soccer stars,

Also jilted his progress and blare,

But go to UAE,

Where he is dearly idolised, if you care –

'A prophet indeed is not honoured

In his own country'

Styles and skills,

He had them in bounty.

If Polo had been a cook,

The aroma from his meals would have wafted

The corridors of all restaurants in Ghana
And beyond,
If Polo had been an architect,
He would have designed
The most glamorous buildings and structures ever,
If Polo had been a designer,
His clothes would been the most stylish and fashionable
For all manner of people to clamour for.
What a player, o what a player!

Dribbling Magician, Scorer of important goals — *these are just two of the numerous accolades my friend and colleague Ken Bediako heaped on Mohammed Polo...Some of us who were fortunate to watch this mercurial footballer develop from his early days till he blossomed into one of the country's greatest stars, were all in agreement that he was and remains Ghana's best-ever.'* **—Joe Aggrey, former Editor, Graphic Sports & Deputy Minister of Sports**

Once the ball is glued to his left foot, it was extremely difficult, if not impossible, to deprive The Soccer Professor of it

Polo – in action ready to perform his magic

The Magician in motion: on the extreme left staying out of reach of an opponent with a body swerve, middle picture getting ready to weave through a number of tackles and on the right getting ready to lay on a tailor-measured pass that is sure to find a colleague.

The Soccer Tactician had a way of accelerating his pace and abruptly applying his breaks to displace and throw his opponents off balance.

Chapter 3

A NEW DAY HAS DAWNED

Sometime in May 1973, I received a letter from my cousin and mentor, Bro. Kaarl NiiOdaai Laye, who used to communicate often with me while I was schooling at Prempeh College in Kumasi. The letter really thrilled my heart.

It read, among others "…A new day has dawned for Hearts. There is a new kid on the block who has taken the entire Hearts team by storm. He has won the hearts of all Hearts fans and has captured the football fraternity around in a whirlwind fashion…"

Even though I do not remember the rest of the story, he succeeded in impressing upon me that a new footballer had arrived on the soccer scene who was going to be the cynosure of all eyes. When I came on holidays and rushed to the training grounds of Hearts at the grassless "Lotteries park" area in Accra around early July, 1973 to watch Ahmed Mohammed play, I was awe-struck, dumbfounded and completely flabbergasted!

Here was a youngster whose pace was astonishing, his passes were flawless, his distribution perfect and his dribbling skills were simply a marvel and a wonder. I think I remember three defenders attempted to mark him that day. These were Addoquaye Addo, Shaibu Fuseini (also a new entrant to Hearts then) and Boye Otinkorang (Moshe Dayan); they were solid and tough defenders who could apply the brakes on any good player. Ahmed Polo made light work of them and run around them with cheeky ease; he made them chase their shadows all afternoon. Ahmed Polo drew applause any time he came into contact with the ball. His skills were beyond compare, even though he was the youngest and smallest in stature compared to his two other colleagues Anas Seidu and Ibrahim Labaran who had just been signed on to play for Auroras, the junior/nursery side of Hearts of Oak as 'new recruits'. After the training session, it took me about one hour to get close enough to offer a handshake. This was because too many people had crowded around the teenager to catch a close glimpse of this emerging football star.

This was the genesis of my encounter with the gem of a football icon that has blown my mind with his sublime skills and, indeed, engraved his name in letters of gold on the football landscape of Ghana, Mohammed Ahmed!

Prior to his arrival, there were football stars who were masters of the game. These included Malik Jabir of Kotoko, Master Dribbler Edwin Conduah of Dwarfs and a Midfield Dynamo in the person of Golden Boy Abdul Razak then of Kumasi Cornerstones. These were all left wingers who, on a good day, could mesmerise defenders and opponents with their dribbling antics and cause fans to applaud them willy-nilly. Other football greats around then, albeit in the twilight of their careers, were Kotoko's 'Generalisimo' Ibrahim Sunday and 'Wizard Dribbler' Osei Kofi, Hearts' 'Slow Motion' Joe Ghartey and Amusa Gbadamosi 'Pele', Cornerstones' Tetteh Gorleku and '99 Styles' Akuetteh Armah as well as Great Olympics' 'Sir' Cecil Jones Attuquayefio. Ahmed Mohammed Polo simply rose head and shoulders above these icons.

*"Polo was the consummate epitome of creativity and vision. With the ball at his feet, it was unequivocal that Polo exhibited the highest quality of the Ghanaian brand of football. There was everything quintessential about Polo's brand of soccer." – **Moses Foh-Amoaning, Veteran Sports Analyst***

'Twins on the field' – Peter Lamptey (Goal Thief) and The Soccer Superamus who fed him with the requisite passes to deliver the goals. He provided all the "assists" for his other team-mates

Chapter 4

EMERGENCE ON THE HEARTS OF OAK SCENE

Polo came to Hearts through the instrumentality of the late avid Colts organizer Skylee and his friend Yushau in 1972. The Dribbling Magician had started his playing career with Bukom/Islamic Stars, Mau Mau and Nima/Kanda Seekers before he was plucked by Hearts. In the words of Oheneba Charles, one of the most respected sports writers Ghana has ever produced, Polo "was the glittering consort of Accra Hearts of Oak and the Black Stars." I have never set eyes on a finer football star, save Argentina's Diego Maradona and Pele of Brazil. The few, to me who come close to him in respect of skills include Raber Madjer of Algeria and perhaps Adolf Armah and Abedi Ayew at the pinnacle of their football careers. The likes of Zidane, Michel Platini, Lionel Messi, Romario, Ronaldinho, David Beckham, Neymar, Rivaldo and their ilk are nowhere near the talent and skill that Polo had. If Polo had displayed his 'soccer-craft' in Europe during his professional days without injury, the world would have woken up to the realization and acknowledgement that Africa has an answer to Pele and Maradona.

Indeed, at the height of his career, Polo and his colleagues in Hearts swept almost every trophy that was to be competed for in Ghana. These included the FA cup, League Cup, Ga Mantse Cup, NRC Cup, Kupyer Cup, SWAG Cup...name them.

The Sports Star magazine in its 20-26th September, 1989 edition had these to write about Polo: 'Mohammed Ahmed Polo is certainly one of the most thoroughbred footballers produced by the continent of Africa. His skills are neither silvery nor golden; they are actually 'diamondic' because his skills are florid: they shine and glitter. In the day time the skills of Polo become the mighty sun which illuminates the skills of the other players and at night, they become the moon which brightens the field where they are… Mohammed Polo is undoubtedly the most talented and the most brilliant player produced by mother Ghana'.

Polo graces the football pitch with such poise and panache that one wonders whether the game of football was not made specifically for him. He so effortlessly controls the ball with the aplomb of a circus juggler that one would love to watch him over and over again without any feeling of boredom. If he chooses to, he can dribble from post-to-post but being an effective team-player he often disposes of a few opponents and lays on millimetre-perfect passes to team-mates. He brought much fun, finesse and flair to the game that even his opponents could not help but admire him during and after matches.

At the time Ahmed Polo burst onto the soccer scene in Ghana, any objective soccer fan could easily identify him as a precocious and budding star who was exceptional in many respects. He had the rare ability of taking on many defenders at a time while running with the ball closely glued to that dangerous and priceless left foot. He could dribble and scheme with tremendous confidence; he had the ability to spot open spaces and made exquisite use of them by exploiting them to his advantage – he either ran into them or made his passes locate only his team-mates there. He was a kaleidoscopic mosaic of many parts whose strengths lay in dribbling, accurate passing, dummying, body swerves and many others all woven into an exquisite tapestry of real soccer artistry. Polo's sleek and silky skills would forever waft through the corridors of Ghanaian stadia for those who watched him and cherish good football for generations to come.

"Technically, I have not seen a more talented and gifted footballer in Ghana than Mohammed Polo. He had everything and is regarded as the best since he announced his presence on the turf in the early 1970s. As an individual, he was an all-round and complete player while in the company of his Hearts colleagues 'The Fearsome Five', they presented the most trenchant and incisive assemblage forward line ever in Ghana football. At a point in time, my colleagues who were sportswriters could not find adequate words to describe him because we had run out of accolades. Some of us decided to call him the 'Soccer Sun'

"The World Eleven" (left) smiling and walking off the pitch after assisting his team to win a match and (right) scaling over a tackle and keeping 'out of coverage area' of an opponent as was his trademark.

Chapter 5

MAGNIFICENCE PERSONIFIED!!!

Polo so mesmerised the entire football-crazy populace and journalists who covered the game that just after displaying the sterling stuff he was made of in his first year as a Hearts player, the Sports Writers Association of Ghana (SWAG) gave him the 'Footballer of The Year' award in 1974. He is the first player to have won that SWAG prize and perhaps the youngest as well.

One of the significant things about Ahmed Polo which I still find very intriguing is his stamina. How could a young boy of his age stay at the far end of the pitch (traditionally he was positioned at the far left corner of the pitch as an outside left/winger), move from there to the midfield to receive passes from team mates, move deep into opponents' midfield to distribute balls with such amazing precision, take effective free-kicks close to opponents' penalty box, dribble deep into opponents' defense, take accurate shots at goal and not tire within 90 minutes? How could he, with his tiny frame, take on so many defenders at a go, ease his way past them as if they did not exist, evade bone-crunching tackles and yet lay on passes so well that he made playing football appear so easy? He displayed these skills for years! How could a player waltz his way around so many opponents with so much effortlessness?

If anybody thought the young lad had only come to exhibit his style and magnificence for a brief period and, like many before him, fade and vanish into thin air for lack of discipline, they were mistaken. His meteoric rise to stardom was no fluke as he stayed and maintained his focus on the field of play for well over 20 years, a feat few footballers can achieve in Ghana. He remained on the plateau of success for decades in spite of injuries that attempted to truncate his career.

In his hey days, fans of Hearts had a way of teasing out defenders and/or opponents any time they attempted to tackle Polo. Fans would chant 'kaaya….kaaya…kaaya' (in the Ga language meaning 'don't go…don't go…don't go' as if to caution the opponent). If the opponent attempted a tackle and was beaten by Polo (which was almost 100% for sure), the fans then responded 'aah, ber workerbo!' meaning 'aah, did we not warn you not to attempt a tackle?'

Indeed, there came a time when defenders of opposing teams dreaded facing a Hearts team that fielded Polo because of how he 'disciplined' them by running rings around them and 'dis-enfranchising' them. Placing a number of defenders on him did not work as he employed innovative and ingenious ways of eluding and evading them.

Polo had a way of adding a touch of class to spice up the game any time he was on the field of play. In my estimation he was to football what Muhammad Ali was to boxing.

Another remarkable thing about Polo was that he had a way of studying his colleagues that made him play to their strength. He brought out the best in strikers and goal-getters e.g. 'Goal Thief' Peter Lamptey, 'Speedster' Kofi Bruce, 'Bomber' Mama Musah 'Acquah', 'Thunder' Anas Seidu, 'Cannon Ball' Tony Tieku, 'Expensive' Robert Hammond ', 'Bayie' Opoku Afriyie, 'Aduro' Opoku Agyeman,' Mueller' Tanko Ayuba and 'Mugu Yaro' Sam Yeboah. On the Black Stars' front he partnered and fed strikers like 'Power House' Kwasi Owusu, 'Soccer Articulator' Agyemang Badu,' Goal Machine' Dan Owusu, George 'Jair' Alhassan and the like.

In spite of his exceptional skills, he was a great team player, always looking out for how he could gel with colleagues for that sharp synergistic impact. It is for that reason that his partnership with schemers like 'Golden Boy' Abdul Razak, 'General' Adolf Armah, 'Papa' Shamo Quaye and the rest made football fans simply relish and savour watching him play over and over again. A keen football enthusiast, Theophilus Morris from the USA, who has been following Ghana football since the 1970s had this to write about Polo - 'he was one player whose ball distribution, dribbling and passing with precision, were at the zenith, without equal' (ref. ghanaweb.com/GhanaHome Page/Sports Archive/Polo Article,206648, 2011).

The late Harry Thompson, one of Ghana's outstanding sports commentators described Ahmed as 'The Polo of Hearts, the Polo of Ghana, the Polo of Africa and the Polo of This World…**olalaaaaa!**!!' (emphasis, mine).

German Coach Karl Heinz Weigang who at various points in time handled Hearts of Oak and the Black Stars in the mid-1970s said of Polo that 'footballers of Polo's type appear once in many generations' and made an offer to The Soccer Superamus to get in touch with him if and when he decided in future to take to coaching. He said he was willing to offer his services to him to the best of his ability adding that it would be unfair if his exceptional skills are not passed on to others.

All in all, Polo played for about 20 years, including many years with Hearts of Oak, professional soccer with Al Wasl (UAE) for 4 years and Shell FC of Gabon for 2 years. Out of a feeling of frustration and ingratitude from Hearts, he featured for rivals Great Olympics for a year or two in the evening of his career. Polo retired from active football in the late 1990s. He has taken to coaching with his own football academy and handled Winneba Advanced Stars, Accra Hearts of Oak and Stade Malien of Mali as well as the youth side of Al Wasl (UAE).

'Assists' In modern football since the game seems to be all about goal-scoring, a 'new' term that has gained currency lately is the importance of 'assists' i.e. the contribution that a player makes to a colleague to score especially if a defender is unable to gain control. In other words, if a pass creates the 'enabling environment' for a colleague to slot in a goal, it is an 'assist'. I dare say that in more than 90% of matches played by Polo, he either played the role of 'assists' in providing the requisite killer-passes to colleagues to score OR when push came to shove, he scored the goal(s) himself. Players of such ilk are rare and appear once in many decades throughout the world. Some football connoisseurs had expected the likes of Emmanuel Duah, Alex Opoku, Daniel Addo, Awudu Issaka, Ablade Kumah, Shamo Quaye and Joe Debrah, as well as some 'latter-day saints' like Christian Atsu, Tarwick Gibril and co. to have blossomed and taken after Polo, the 'Soccer Superamus' but this dream has not seen the light of day.

Describing him, sportswriter M. B. Brimah in the 24th September, 1974 edition of *Sports Digest* had this to say of Ahmed Polo:

"...He lays on goal chances for team-mates in a variety of ways...has a skill that is demonstrated in his first-time distribution, his delicate flicks for a supporting colleague running through a defense looking for a return pass, and by dribbling past defenders with cheeky ease and then realising that he is at too fine an angle to shoot himself, pulling back for a well-placed colleague to shoot at the full face of the goal...Polo's intelligence, perception and simple unselfishness combine with his natural talents to make him one of the most dangerous winger-strikers in the game... though perhaps only those who play alongside him fully realise his true value...in possession of the ball anywhere on the pitch, Polo is one of the few players who can decide what to do with the ball at any time, taking defenders on, feinting and bobbing, dribbling past one opponent after another until he decides what else to do with the ball... Polo's left foot is indeed gifted. He is quick too, decisive in his passing and exciting in his dribbling ability. He is an intelligent, constructive footballer with elegance and instinct for creating the goal chances and giving satisfaction to the fans. Polo is a figure second to none in Ghana football."

Sam Johnson, one of Hearts of Oak's great utility players said of Polo that whenever you played alongside Polo, it was as though your side had 13 players as compared to the opposing side's 11; the implication was that Polo played as if he alone had attributes that made him "three-players embodied in one person."

Professional Soccer in The US That Never Was

Sometime in 1977 Willie Evans, a dire-hard Hearts of Oak fan and defender who had played for the Black Stars and/or Real Republicans and who was plying his trade in the USA came to Ghana in an attempt lure Mohammed Polo and Peter Lamptey to play professional soccer there. At that time both players, being integral part of the famous 'Fearsome Five' were instrumental in the success story of Hearts. Peter Lamptey had won the SWAG 'goal-king' award in 1975 with 23 goals while Ahmed Polo had annexed the 'Footballer of The Year' award in 1974. When fans heard about the proposed trip to the US by the two footballers, they, in anger, stalled the plan and allegedly beat up Willie Evans, the agent, accusing him of sabotage. They felt he was being **disloyal** to the club because it was going to be difficult for Hearts to make progress and thrive in the absence of the two soccer stars. One of the directors of Hearts, Nii Amarh Armarteifio accused Willie Evans of betrayal. The two were prevented from signing the contract that would have linked them to professional soccer in the US. Later it was learnt that the then head of state, General Kutu Acheampong was in support of the plan that scuttled the US trip and was rumoured to have remarked that Polo and Peter were 'non-exportable commodities' for Ghana. (Sam Doku, *Graphic Sports*, June 18-23, 1991 edition)

What more can be said about this gem of a footballer?

"'Polo is one of the best footballers the nation has produced. Initially he engaged in too much fanciful dribbling, in my estimation, but as he matured he became a good passer of the ball and scored a lot of goals himself."
— Assad Mallah, Veteran football Administrator of Asante Kotoko

Celebrated Sportswriter Ken Bediako took this with Polo in Dar Es Salaam, Tanzania in 1974 after a champion league quarter final match between Hearts of Oak and Simba Club. It ended 0-0.

Ken and Polo were close companions during matches (whether 'home' or 'away')

Flashback, 1977: Willie Evans (former Ghanaian international) and Nii Adjiri Blanskon (former Accra Mayor) posing with Peter Lamptey and Ahmed Polo while they append their signatures to contracts that were going to link them to play professional football in the USA. The deal was scuttled at the last minute.

Chapter 6

SELECTED MEMORABLE MATCHES

Hearts-Akotex, FA Cup, Accra,1977

Akotex, a factory-owned club (belonging to Akosombo Textiles Ltd.) had stormed the elite football division with amazing success in the mid-1970s. In the 1977 FA cup competition, Akotex dismissed all opposition to meet Hearts in the final. Parading dreaded firebrands like Adjei in goal, in defense Michel Lomo, Tanko Gibrine 'Rozo', Anthony Dwemoh, a well-oiled midfield of Eric Amankwah, Thomas Kankam, Eric Kodi, Gogo Amoah and spearheaded by a trenchant forward-line of Oheneba Siaw, Sintim Aboagye and Yaw Mark, Akotex harassed Hearts and were coasting to a 2-1 victory. Polo had been busy all night (the match was played in late afternoon and under floodlights when it was getting dark) as usual feeding his colleagues with accurate passes. When all appeared lost and fans of Hearts were trooping from the stadium in disappointment with the conclusion that 'well, the FA cup belongs to Akotex this year, so let them have it, anyway.... their victory is well-deserved', Polo struck on the stroke of full time. He fetched the equaliser with a fierce right-footed shot bringing the final score to 2-2 after dribbling past a forest of legs. He had played the match with so much glee, guile and gusto that it would have been a travesty of justice if he had been on the losing side. Since there had to be a winner, the match was re-scheduled to a later date. Hearts won that match 2-0 through the influence of the 'Magic' Polo again.

Hearts-Lions (Benin), Accra, 1985

In 1985, Hearts participated in the Africa Cup Championship competition. The club was fortunate to have registered some of the players who had returned from playing professional soccer abroad, including Polo and Adolf Armah. Polo made all the difference in the Hearts set-up when the team faced the Lions of Benin in late March, beating them 3-0 in the first leg at the Accra Sports stadium. Below is how celebrated sportswriter Oheneba Charles captured events:

"Look at the way he chests the ball…look at the way he made the opponent's defense break into an undignified scramble any time he felt like it…look at the easy way he thrusted through the flailing arms of the Lions defenders…look at the effortless manner in which he distributed his passes…look at his deft body swerves and deadly accurate back-heels which almost always left the opponents trailing despairingly in his shadow… look at his athleticism, authority, confidence and sureness of touch any time he entered the fringe range…look at the power behind his shots…look at his inter-positional play…look at the easy way he avoided the clattering and crunching tackles…oh look at the way he made goal-scoring look so easy and simple…Those are the beautiful lessons taught by "Professor" Ahmed Polo, the glittering god of Ghana football when he re-appeared on the local scene (after almost eight years' absence) to feature for his mother club, Accra Hearts of Oak in their crucial second leg Africa Cup Championship preliminary match against the Lions Club of Benin at the Accra Sports Stadium last *Sunday*."' (*The Sporting Times*, Vol. No. 6, March 26-April 1, 1985)

In that match, Polo scored two beautiful goals and set up the other for Opoku Afriyie to send fans into wild jubilation and a frenzy for days and weeks. That day, I felt deep in my heart that such skills needed to be showcased at the World Cup stage and not be limited to football-crazy fans in Accra.

The celebrated sports writer was later to describe Polo as someone who taught soccer lessons to stubborn defenders and "making them look silly … his goals were impossible to describe" (Oheneba Charles, *Boxing Football Illustrated*, No. 0007A, May/June, 1985).

Later, in describing Polo further, he remarked that he "…was noted for the way he softened opponent's defence with superb dribbling…the gazelle-like pace, the thoughtful penetration, the flamboyance, the sureness of touch, the deadly accurate back-heels, the delicate flicks, the on-the-peg passes….make him the superstar of yesteryears." (Oheneba Charles, *The Sports World*, August, 1985)

The Mega Star getting ready to display his antics on an opponent

Black Stars-Nigeria, Nigeria, 1975

I remember a match between Black Stars and Nigeria in Surulere (played under floodlights) in August, 1975 during the Ghana-Nigeria Friendship Games. The Green Eagles (as they were called then) took an early lead and held on doggedly for long. Polo kept laying on tailor-measured passes to his team mates and strikers upfront after disposing of a number of defenders time and again all evening. For the entire 90 minutes, the Green Eagles, though leading by a lone goal, were reeling under pressure any time Polo took control of the ball. He employed body swerves, feinting and his usual dribbling antics to dance his way out of tackles and kept feeding his colleagues with balls upfront to no avail. A minute before full time, he decided to take on the entire defense himself and succeeded in scoring a timely equaliser to bring the match to a deadlock (1-1). Children and adults flocked round him after the match like bees settling on nectar to congratulate him for his magic and wizardry. After other matches played between the Black Stars and Green Eagles, the then skipper of the Nigerian team, Christian Chukwu who was a pillar in the Nigerian defense, when asked to describe Polo, replied that he was the 'Defenders' Nightmare'. This was due to the way he took on defenders and made his way past them with so much ease no matter how closely they attempted to neutralise him. He was simply too difficult to police or mark in a match.

...with his colleagues Tony Micah, Robert Hammond, Evans Aryee Quaye and co. celebrating a victory very characteristic of their time.

Black Stars-Morocco, Kumasi, 1975

During an African Nations Cup qualifying match played in Kumasi on 29th June, 1975, Polo again was in good company with colleagues like Joe Sam, Opoku Afriyie and Abdul Razak. All afternoon, Polo captivated the entire Kumasi stadium with his amazing skills, cutting easily through the Moroccan midfield and defense. He succeeded in winning a penalty after being brought down, having dismissed some four defenders in a row and almost on his way to scoring in one of his dangerous moves. There was not a ball that Polo kicked that had any flaw associated with it – passes, timing of his movements, corner kicks, free-kicks, dribbling etc. The Black Stars eventually won the match 2-0 in that Africa Cup of Nations/World Cup qualifying match. The Moroccan players and officials stared in awe and were speechless after the match, struggling to fathom how they had been humiliated in Kumasi by the Black Star via the instrumentality of *The Dribbling Magician*. That day, an elderly football fan who was watching the match on television with me remarked 'What an exceptionally gifted player. I have never seen anybody play football with so much skill, ease and finesse! I can liken him to Pele. What Pele was to Santos and Brazil, Polo is to Hearts and Ghana!'

Black Stars-Guinea, Conakry, 1985

In another Africa Nations Cup qualifying match played in Conakry, Guinea on 14th April, 1985 the Black Stars had been playing fairly well, especially capturing of the midfield where Polo was operating in partnership with Sampson Lamptey, Abedi Ayew, George Lamptey and co. After the Black Stars went up 1-0, the Guineans equalised and appeared to have been recovering, with the fans rallying behind them. The Black Stars lifted their game and scored again. Being 2-1 down, the Guineans again attempted to improve their play with the expectation that being one-goal down was not too big a deal. Polo and his colleagues replied by organising a very fluid game in midfield. He scored the third goal to put the game beyond recovery and cooked a wonder of a goal for Abedi Ayew to bring the final results to 4-1.

This was how the last goal came about. When the Black Stars earned a corner kick or the ball was sent to the left side of the Guinean defense area, everybody expected the floating of the ball into the heavily packed penalty box. Polo, instead, floated a long ball from the corner spot area way outside the penalty box towards the middle of the field. Watching the match, for a moment I wondered whether he had made a mistake. The ball eventually landed on the itching left foot of Abedi Ayew who volleyed it straight into the net. It sent the entire stadium to sleep as people kept wondering what kind of stuff Polo and his colleagues were made of. His ball-sense was unimaginable. Black Stars won the away match by a 4-1 margin in faraway Monrovia. He had become the mentor and inspirer of the young and budding star Abedi Ayew 'Pele'. Abedi was later to confess that Ahmed Polo was his mentor and that it was a pity that he was not able to learn all his skills before embarking on his professional career in Europe. Abedi Pele says that Ahmed Polo was and has been his mentor; "Polo was my idol. He was everything to me. When I see Polo playing, it was just magical. The way he moves through, the way he gives his body swerves, the way he runs…I was glued at the stadium watching Polo" adding that he regrets not having succeeded in learning all the skills Polo had during his football career (www.Ghanagossip.com).

Black Stars-Libya, Benghazi, 1985

Even though Ghana lost this match 0-2 to Libya that was played on an unfamiliar artificial pitch in this World Cup qualifying match played in faraway Benghazi on 26th July, 1985, Polo distinguished himself extremely well, having flown in from UAE a day before the match. He kept feeding colleagues Opoku Nti ('Tarkwa Polo'), George Alhassan and colleagues as usual with his near-perfect passes. He was unlucky not to have been on the winning team. His distribution was excellent even though he did not dribble much on the day due to stamina challenges.

Realising his conditioning was not at its zenith, he conserved energy by sending prompt and ready passes to his colleagues, exploiting holes in their defensive set-up and making use of open spaces.

Other matches in which Polo excelled include Black Stars against The Elephants of Cote d'Ivoire during a World Cup qualifying match; against Liberia, Senegal, Tunisia, Uganda and Gambia. He was capped more than 50 times by the national team IN SPITE OF HIS INJURIES.

1977, Africa Clubs Championship Cup, Quarter Final match (Hearts-El Ahly, 0-0, Egypt), 3-0, Accra

In the first leg of the one-eighth finals of the Africa Cup for champion clubs, Hearts lost by a lone goal to El Ahly of Egypt. Polo played as a half-fit player for the entire game. Owing to his ill-health, he could not operate at optimum level even though, as usual, he succeeded in creating a few openings in the defense of El Ahly for his team mates. He drilled some holes in their defense with his incisive passes and dribbling antics.

Even though Hearts did not win the match, Polo was voted the "man-of the-match". Indeed, after that match, there were rumours that the Egyptians had found out that Polo was a Muslim and attempted to 'kidnap' him. The plan was to keep him in Egypt in order to prevent him from featuring in the return leg or try to persuade him to change clubs later to join El Ahly.

In the second leg played in Accra, Polo was rested in the first half since he was still yet to fully recuperate from the injury that had kept him from operating at full throttle in the first leg. He studied the game from the sidelines like a tactician, during which time Hearts struggled for an elusive goal. It appeared the Hearts team was bereft of ideas, because there were too many stray passes, few shots at goal, inertia and general lack of cohesion. Fans were getting jittery and disappointed. Some supporters of Hearts started leaving the stadium during recess.

Then, Polo stepped into the game in the second half. He suddenly changed the tempo, pace and character of the Hearts team. The fans responded by chanting his name and singing Hearts' anthem. As usual, he exploited spaces in midfield and started feeding his colleagues with tailor-measured passes that punched holes into the defense of El Ahly. Even though the coach of El Ahly kept shouting to his players, particularly the defenders, to hold Polo in check, the Dribbling Magician was too hot to handle.

Polo floated and cruised on the field like an eel, moving with grace, class and elegance to the delight of the entire stadium. He succeeded in helping Hearts to win by a tidy 3-0 margin to move into the semi-finals of the continental competition that year. Polo was just the perfect elixir for the club to eliminate their feared opponents from North Africa.

Miracle Of El Wak, 1977, Africa Clubs Championship Cup, Semi-Final match

Owing to injury, Polo had missed the first leg of the semi-final match in Zambia. Hearts had lost the match 2-5 in Kitwe. The Zambian club had succeeded in eliminating the mighty Mouloudia club of Algeria at the quarter final stage and had a very formidable team. Many analysts wrote Hearts off, but the die-hard fans filled the El Wak stadium to capacity to provide moral support. It was tough because Hearts needed at least three unanswered goals against the dreaded Zambians to proceed to the finals. The match was played at the El Wak stadium owing to renovation works at the Accra Sports stadium in preparation for the 1978 Africa Cup of Nations' cup which Ghana was going to host.

'Hearts of Oak played a miraculous second half, scoring three goals without reply in the last 20 minutes of the game to register a 3-0 win over the tough Zambian side…and who now doubts that Mohammed Polo is Hearts of Oak? The 22-year-old Nima-born Dribbling Magician made all the difference in the Hearts' team,' wrote veteran Sports writer Ken Bediako of the *Daily Graphic.*

"For the 90 minutes that Polo featured in the return leg, it was as if he had just descended from the heavens to showcase a novel brand of football on earth. Again, he was the nexus around which the entire game revolved. He initiated attacks, took the set pieces, fed his colleagues as usual with inch-perfect tailor-measured passes, flew past his opponents with supersonic pace, caused havoc in the opponents' penalty box any time he had the ball and, indeed, lit the entire stadium with his magic wand.

"One of the Zambian radio commentators was heard asking whether Polo was human. To him, what Polo displayed that day was from outer space; he was simply magnificent. Polo assisted Hearts to win the match 3-0 in what has become known as the *'Miracle of El Wak'*. He had a hand in all the three goals that Hearts scored that day to qualify them for the finals of the Africa clubs championship. On the 90th minute, with Hearts leading by 2-0 and having exhibited all that there was in the game, Polo once again ensured that Hearts reached the finals by providing that extra explosion of genius. He meandered his way past some three defenders and sent a defense-splitting pass to 'Bomber' Mama Acquah who in turn sent it to the itching feet of 'Thunder' Anas Seidu to easily slot in the much-awaited goal. Polo was carried shoulder-high by Hearts' fans amid wild jubilation deep into the night," ended Ken Bediako's report (*Daily Graphic*, 7th November, 1977).

Owing to injury, he could not feature in the two-leg final matches. Hearts lost the African cup painfully to Hafia Club of Guinea that year. Many fans believe that, had Polo played in those two matches, Hearts could and most probably would have won the Africa championship cup as far back as 1977.

Hearts-Kotoko, June 4th Anniversary Cup match, 1990/91

When the league season ends in Europe, most Ghanaian footballers return home to rest. These are moments when most professional footballers take a good respite from their hectic schedules abroad. The disciplined ones engage in light exercises and occasional friendly matches in order to keep fit and not get rusty. Polo had come to Ghana on vacation from the UAE where he had been playing professional soccer.

The Dribbling Professor decided to introduce another dimension of sheer panache from his football inventory. Realising that the little extra weight was going to impact on his stamina, he decided not to run nor be as mobile as his normal self. He chose not to stay at his favourite traditional left-wing area (outside left) either. Polo decided to operate from the centre of midfield right in front of the defenders. Once he got possession of the ball, he just walked and sprayed passes to team-mates in different directions. It was simply splendid.

Even when he had to dribble, as had always been his hallmark, he would not hurry but take his time, rely on feinting, body swerves to outwit his opponents and make use of open spaces in the Kotoko defense. He succeeded in setting up his colleagues to blast in two quick goals within the first half for the match to eventually end 2-1 in Hearts' favour.

Polo's delight that day was just to take possession, lay on passes at short intervals – interlaced and tinged with occasional long passes – and just walk around his opponents while keeping the ball within his reach only and away from them as if to tease them. At the end of the day, a celebrated sports journalist commented that Polo had used his **'walking soccer'** strategy to outmaneuver the entire Kotoko outfit. It was amazing that even an over-weight Polo could rely on his wizardry to take complete control of the midfield that day, over-shadowing his younger Kotoko opponents and succeeding in stealing the show.

Indeed, if the Hearts strikers had taken their chances well, Hearts would have won that match by a much wider margin. After the match, fans of Hearts carried him shoulders high and pleaded with him not to return to Al Wasl his club in the UAE.

1978 Black Stars Squad, Africa Cup of Nations' Finals hosted by Ghana

Ahmed Polo picked up a nagging injury in 1976 that nearly truncated his football career. So disturbing was the injury that he was nearly left out of the Black Stars squad that hosted the Africa Cup of Nations' Finals staged here in Ghana. Indeed, it took the singular intervention of the then Head of State, General Kutu Acheampong through his Special Assistant in charge of Sports, Lt. Col. Simpe Asante, to plead earnestly for the Soccer Superamus to agree, willy-nilly, to feature for the Black Stars.

General Acheampong felt a half-fit Polo playing for just 45 minutes was enough to drill holes in the defense of any team. Indeed he contributed a lot for Ghana to win the cup for keeps. Polo had to sacrifice and dig deep into the rare virtues of nationalism, patriotism and loyalty – at the peril of his life – to play for Ghana.

Even in that state, he together with his compatriots succeeded in lifting the Africa Cup for keeps and was named among the four Ghanaians in the CAF Team of the tournament, alongside Kuuku Dadzie, Adolf Armah and Abdul Razak who was voted Africa's '*Best Footballer*' that year. Perhaps if Polo had been fit, he could have easily won that title.

At the group stages of that competition, Polo assisted Ghana to beat then Upper Volta (now Burkina Faso) by scoring a goal while providing the ammunition ('assist') to compatriot George Alhassan to score two. He played in almost all the matches in a half-fit state of health but was quite excited and thrilled to sacrifice for mother Ghana. That was the hallmark of genuine patriotism and nationalism! It is a pity that the estate houses promised the team by the then Head of State was never honoured nor fulfilled.

> *"To me Polo was the greatest player after the Brazilian Pele generation. The only player to match him was Diego Maradona. I don't think even Messi or Ronaldo can match his football skills and talent."* **– Ben Ephson, Former Editor of Afro Sports**

Polo (even as an injured player) joins his Black Stars colleagues to celebrate the historic victory by winning the Africa Cup of Nations cup for the third time in 1978 in Ghana.

Chapter 7

REMARKABLE ACHIEVEMENTS

Polo was the first and perhaps youngest footballer to be awarded the *Footballer of The Year* title in 1974 by the Sports Writers Association of Ghana.

Polo is one of the few footballers (I know of only three) who floated a corner kick that zoomed straight into an opponent's net for a goal. This was between Hearts of Oak and Susu Biribi in a 1974 league match at Accra Stadium on May 4, 1974.

When, in 2006, Ghana won a place to participate in the World Cup Finals in Germany among 23 other countries, a special competition was held by FIFA and Coca Cola, one of the sponsors of the tournament. Polo was voted the most outstanding player and was honoured with the novelty 'Breaking Down Barriers' award. The award was for retired international players who have used the game as a means to foster peace among people of different ethnic and religious persuasions as well as those who have succeeded in rising from lowly beginnings, using football as a form of encouragement to many especially the financially-challenged. He and other retired players like Odartey Lamptey played a match in Tamale to ease tension amid the Komkomba-Nanumba ethnic clashes in late 2005 and early 2006.

Polo was the first Ghanaian/African to have won the Best Player of the season award in the UAE in 1979/80.

Polo and Edward 'Santrofi' Acquaah are on record to be the youngest players ever to captain Accra Hearts of Oak. Polo entered the big stage at about 17/18 years of age and succeeded in making a name that became second to none in Ghana for decades.

Polo is also credited to be among the few players to have played active football for more than 20 years both in Ghana and beyond (UAE and Gabon) – in spite of all the injuries he had to contend with – before quitting the game. He featured among the likes of 'Afro' Joe Dakota, Henry Lante 'Duru' France, 'Slow Motion' Joe Ghartey, Tetteh Chandu in the early 1970s, hit the apogee of success with 'Bomber' Mama Musah 'Acquah', 'Expensive' Robert Hammond, 'Goal Thief Peter Lamptey and 'Thunder' Anas Seidu as the **The Fearsome Fivesome** in the late 70s and ended with 'latter-day saints' like 'Papa' Shamo Quaye, Ablade Kumah, and Joe Amoateng in the mid-1990s.

Polo appears to be the player with the highest number of accolades in the history of Ghana football. His appellations include **'Dribbling Professor', 'Scorer of Important**

Goals', 'Soccer Calculator', 'Dribbling Magician', 'Soccer Emeritus', 'Soccer Professor', 'Soccer Virtuoso', 'World Eleven', 'Soccer Scientist', 'Soccer Tactician', 'Soccer Superamus', 'Wonder Boy', 'Soccer Emperor', 'Soccer Craftsman', 'Soccer Sun', 'Soccer Engineer', 'Game Changer', 'Soccer Emperor', 'Wizard Dribbler', 'Soccer Maestro' and many more, which time and space would not allow us to enumerate.

Polo was so good many players wanted either to be like him or used his name as a prefix to theirs. For instance, Opoku Nti of Asante Kotoko fame was affectionately called 'Tarkwa Polo' before he graduated to become Zico; Godfried Aduobe of Kotobabi Powerlines who grew to ply his trade abroad was nick-named 'UK Polo' while Nii Moi, a rising star then was called 'Nima Polo'. Other youngsters like 'Under -17' icon Awudu Issaka and Tarwick Gibril were both tagged with Polo's name and fame.

THE 'FEARSOME FIVESOME' & COLLEAGUES

Polo and his four colleagues who lined up in the forward-line of Hearts of Oak were referred to as The Fearsome Five. They and the rest of their colleagues who dominated Ghana's football scene in the early 1970s and 1980s are described below.

Mama Musah burst into the limelight in the 1970s with lightning pace and a sound combination of strength and skill. It is no wonder that he was given the nickname 'Nima Jet'. 'Bomber' was however his popular name. He had ferocious shots in both feet and was also vey stylish. He later became the skipper of the club having gained a call-up to the Black Stars around 1970 alongside others like Kwasi Owusu, Malik Jabir, John Eshun, and Henry 'Duru' Lante France. Mama Musah was a very good rallying point for both players and fans as he used his popularity and enigma to calm nerves when the going got tough for the club. He became very loyal to the club, was a dedicated player with leadership acumen and under his captainship Hearts won many laurels. *(May the soul of Mama Musah rest in peace!)*

Robert Hammond had a number of other names such as 'Mikey Ronney', 'Expensive' and 'Mr. Web Offset'. He was a wily utility player who could use both feet effectively, hence could play in many different positions except goalkeeping and in defense. Though not having a fast pace, he could dribble and scheme as well as strike occasionally. Robert Hammond could also make use of his head in a dexterous manner to beat goalkeepers. Even though Accra Gt. Olympics succeeded in poaching him for a year at the height of his career, he made a quick U-turn the following year to join his four other colleagues in a partnership attack that has seen no equal in Ghana soccer. *(May the soul of Robert Hammond rest in peace!)*

'Goal Thief' **Peter Lamptey** was snatched from rivals Gt. Olympics in 1972 at a time when he was known as 'Bukom

Pele'. The remarkable thing about Peter, also called 'Avalon', was that aside his dribbling skills and astonishing pace, he had a special eye for goals. He could turn half-chances into goals at the least opportunity. "Whenever Peter Lamptey is lurking around your goal area, one should not make a mistake of being careless with defending; he could pounce on the slightest error and score from the most acute of angles," a stalwart defender once said about him. On the field of play, it was as if Peter Lamptey was always thinking about how best to outwit a goalkeeper. Many of his goals came through sheer skill and wit rather than from firing in terrific shots. Peter was the first player to win the SWAG goal-king title in 1973/4 with 26 goals. He was drafted into the national team in 1971 and took part in a number of international assignments including the Olympic Games in Munich in 1972. He had to play second fiddle to the likes of Kwasi and Dan Owusu as strikers in the Black Stars.

Anas Seidu, popularly called 'Thunder', joined Hearts in 1971 as a youngster. Owing to his bulky and burly stature, he could bulldoze his way through many defenders and tackles to score goals. He had a high rate of conversion of spot kicks as he hardly missed a penalty. Anas had tremendous shots in both feet. On a few occasions that he missed the net with his shots hitting the crossbar, they shook the very foundations of the goal posts; the weak ones got uprooted from the sheer force that accompanied the shots. It was rumoured that in a fiercely contested match between Hearts and Kotoko, once upon a time, the force from one of his free kicks tore the jersey of

Goalkeeper Paul Ayoma and got him substituted from an accompanying injury, thus earning Anas Seidu the name 'Ayooma Killer'. He was a member of the Black Stars that won the Africa Cup of Nations' cup on home soil in 1978 even though not a regular. He later played professional soccer in the UAE and Gabon, like his close compatriot Ahmed Polo.

These five guys (Polo included) were ably supported by the following players at the height of his football career in the mid 1970s:

'Super' Sam Suppey was a goalkeeper who was plucked from Brong Ahafo United in 1975. He was a fearless and dependable goalie whose anticipation was very good; he exhibited sharp reflexes and could pull off some dramatic saves with sheer bravado. His physique was a sound mix of some bulk and agility that made him a pillar in the post. Sam displayed a great deal of confidence in very sticky situations that helped prevent balls from entering his net.

Ofei Ansah was one of the most ruthless and hard-nosed defenders Ghana has ever had. He was a tough player who played the game with enormous passion and power both on the ground and in the air with crunching slide tackles and heavy body-checks. His main aim was to apply breaks on any attacker, and he employed fair and foul means to achieve that objective. He was very good at converting free kicks and spot kicks. Ofei was a member of the Black Stars that won the Africa Nations'

Cup in Ghana in 1978.

Evans Aryeequaye was a calm but effective left-full back who relied very much on his skills to outwit his opponents. He came to Hearts from Sekondi Hassacas in 1976 and was difficult to beat. He could overlap cleverly and provided safe haven for the team, having been the skipper of the Academicals (made up of students in tertiary institutions in Ghana) for quite a while.

Nii Noi Thompson, Sarpei Nunoo and Seth Ampadu were unyielding half-backs who were good on the ground and in the air. They were very tough and could put fear into opposing players with their timely clearances and lateral marking to mount an impregnable barrier at the rear for Hearts of Oak with abundant display of stamina, resilience and fortitude. Anthony 'Seaman' Micah was the pivot of the Hearts defense. This bearded steely bloke was hard in all departments of the game. With the heart of a lion, he simply would not allow an opponent to get past him. Coming from the Western Region, he employed a combination of close-marking and timely clearances to ensure that his goal area was safe with gritty determination.

Adolf Armah, 'The Generalissimo', was introduced into the Hearts team around 1977 after the exit of 'afro-haired' Tetteh Chandu who himself had taken over from 'Mr. Slow Motion' Joe Ghartey. Having started with the likes of Tanko Ayuba, Jesse Mallet and Abdul Kadri Baba Gambo, he rose to become a very fine link between the Hearts defense and forward-line. The skills of Adolf became so honed that he became not only a member of the Black Stars that won the African Cup for keeps in 1978, he later became the skipper of the Black Stars and was voted second African Best Player in 1979 by CAF. With admirable body swerves and some dribbling antics, Adolf's ball distribution was superb.

Some other players who assisted this formidable team were goalkeepers Paul Annan, Sannie Abudulai, Owusu Mensah and many more, defenders 'My Son' Sam Amarteifio, Boye Sowah 'Tuule', Addoquaye, Shaibu Hasaf Fuseini, Boye 'Moshe Dayan' Otinkorang, 'No Way' Hesse Odamtten and Yusifu Salifu, midfielders Bismark Odoi and Douglas Tagoe as well as Tanko Ayuba, a young striker.

Fearsome Five (Unfortunately, the fifth person 'Expensive' Robert Hammond was off camera because he had to consult a pressman urgently just before the photograph was taken)

From left: 'Bomber' Mama Musah Acquah, 'Dribbling Magician' Ahmed Polo, 'Goal Thief' Peter Lamptey and 'Thunder Anas Seidu

"Polo is the most technically gifted player this nation has ever produced… if he had played in Europe, no player could have compared with him and he would have had no peers. If he had also gone through a soccer academy similar to what Lionel Messi benefitted from, he would have had no equal; he was exceptional in many ways. Polo was better than Messi and could do amazing things beyond imagination with the ball." – **Veteran Coach J. E. Sarpong**

Chapter 8

PROFESSIONAL SOCCER

Ahmed Polo can be described as a legend who played for Al Wasl for four years from 1979 to 1982. He made goal-scoring easy for strikers owing to the way he placed or directed his passes. Polo helped his club Al Wasl to win the league title for the first time in its history in 1979 after he joined the team that same year. He assisted his team to win the league titles again in 1980, 1981 and 1982.

It was reported in 2006, after a survey among soccer-fans and journalists, that Mohammed Ahmed Polo was selected as the Best Foreign Player of all time in the history of UAE soccer. This was because fans felt that he displayed outstanding and unparalleled skills during his four seasons with Al Wasl FC. It was reported, among others, that Polo's memory remains alive in the hearts of the fans…his name is still mentioned frequently. Polo was a talented world-class player and was unlucky not to have exhibited his style in the early 1980s in Europe because the continent was yet to open its doors wide to

African players. But for this, Polo would have easily played for some of Europe's biggest clubs.

The report goes on to mention that not only was he a great footballer but also a tactician on the field of play. It continued "nobody has ever comprehended how he scored the goal in the final match against the Gulfans. It was done 'Maradona-style'. He dribbled past five Gulf players, scaled the ball over the head of (Goalkeeper) Fahd Khamees, then scored the most expensive league winning goal that gave Al Wasl its second consecutive champions league victory in 1981." (*Al-Ittihad Riyaada*, Leading newspaper, UAE, 23/08/2006, translated from Arabic)

According to sportswriter Sam Doku, "…back then Mohammed Polo, the best thing to have happened to Ghana soccer…stunned the Saudi Arabian populace such that they were left dumbfounded making them wonder if his feet did not have any supernatural magnetic powers." (*Graphic Sports*, June 18-23, 1991 edition)

Gabon

Close to the twilight of his career, Ahmed Polo was poached by the late Ghanaian Coach Ben Kuoffie to ply his trade with Shell Football Club in Gabon between 1986 and 1989. The coach, who had been a good footballer himself and had played for the Black Stars/Republicans during President Nkrumah's reign, was scouting for quality players to build the newly-formed young football club. Even though Polo could not help Shell FC to win any memorable cups in the Gabonese league, he played a key role in lifting the club to rub shoulders with the elites at that time e.g. FC105, AS Sogara and Petrosport. Indeed, many years after leaving the shores of Gabon, some football managers and soccer connoisseurs still recollect his amazing skills and contact him in Ghana for help when looking out for talents to groom.

> *"It was a big honour and privilege to play alongside this gem of a footballer. Time and space would not allow me to recount how special and exceptional he was. He brought a touch of class to the game [more] than anybody else I have ever encountered." –* **Evans Aryeequaye, Defender & Colleague, June 2019**

> "Ahmed Polo was exceptional in many respects. With his pace and dribbling skills, one was scared as a defender to tackle him because it was very difficult to mark him. Such skills are rare and the nation should honour such outstanding and remarkable personalities who made the game click and captured the hearts of many fans." – ***Kwasi Appiah, former Kotoko defender, Black Stars team-mate & later Black Stars Coach, May 2019 (Kantanka TV interview)***

"I started playing football with Polo at a tender age. Polo is naturally-gifted, the reason why he could do exceptional things with the ball. He was so talented that whenever I played alongside him, I was perfectly at ease because he knew how to lay on the requisite passes to me that would make me score goals. The vibe and telepathy between the two of us was superb. Together, we mesmerised all the teams we came into contact with in our hey-days." — **'Thunder' Anas Seidu, May 2019**

Officials and scouts from the UAE pose with Polo and Peter after the first leg of the Hearts-Al Ahly match in Egypt, 1976/7. Hearts lost the match 0-1 but redeemed themselves in the second leg with an emphatic 3-0 victory in Accra.

Chapter 9

HICCUPS

Being human, the Soccer Superamus encountered some challenges to his career. Here are three challenges that nearly marred Polo's entire football career.

Injuries

Owing to the flamboyance and colourful nature of his play that left defenders dazed and flattened, many made conscious and deliberate attempts to crush those mesmerising feet. It is only to the glory of God that Polo was able to evade many real bone-shackling tackles that would have crippled him.

In spite of his pace, smartness and agility that made him escape many of those wicked tackles, few got to him occasionally. For about fifteen out of the twenty years of his playing life, Polo had to be nursing a nagging groin injury as well as a torn ligament in his right foot. Those injuries nearly ruled him out of the Black Stars squad that hosted (and won) the 1978 Africa Cup of Nations on home soil. Had it not been for that groin injury, Polo and his team-mates, 'The Fearsome Fivesome', backed by the likes of Goalkeeper 'Super' Sam Suppey, Ofei 'O'

Ansah, Evans Aryeequaye, Nii Noi Thompson, Tony 'Seaman' Micah and Adolf Armah would and could have won the Clubs Championship Cup for Hearts in 1977.

Disaffection from Management

Did you know that at the peak of his football career, Polo had to be taking medications of various kinds on many occasions just to make him fit enough to feature for Hearts in crucial matches? In a few instances, when the predicament was unbearable, Polo requested Hearts' authorities to allow him to go and seek 'alternative treatment' from local sources .This did not go down well with some Hearts' top officials who unfortunately branded him as uncooperative and intransigent. This, at times, unfortunately brought him on collision courses with former Hearts' late Chairman Tommy Thompson and some Black Stars management members.

Prophet Theory

Having been plucked and nurtured by Hearts of Oak, the club and their numerous admirers have always seen Polo as a born and bred 'Phobian'. Many who saw his meteoric rise to stardom as a player predicted he could become a top-class coach in the future. True to the prediction and deep affection for Hearts, Polo attempted to impart his rich football skills to younger players through coaching. On the three occasions that Polo was asked to handle Hearts, he tried his best. Strangely enough, some detractors labelled him as a non-starter with questionable technical skills. They saw him as 'the young prodigy from Nima' instead of regarding him as 'the Soccer Professor who had come of age'. Such 'supporters' tried various 'ways and means' to malign and deliberately drown his efforts to become a successful coach.

"Any time I come to think of Polo, I wish that he would have displayed his skills at the World Cup stage for football-loving fans to really appreciate that Ghana has talents. He knew how to play so well without being taught by anybody that one wonders whether he did not invent the game himself. I admired him so much so that I had to make a conscious effort to only watch the openings he created for me as a striker; I looked out for the gaps he created in our opponents' defense and simply had to exploit them to our advantage. Playing alongside Polo made goal-scoring easy. He was my most cherished companion on the field of play because I was assured that, with him in my squad, a goal from me was guaranteed." – Goal Thief' Peter Lamptey, June 2019

"Mohammed Polo was for me one of the best footballers I have come across and had the privilege to play with. What could a coach teach him? He knew what to do with the ball and how to do it. Indeed, he was such a skillful player that even if a coach succeeded in teaching him a particular thing, he had the ability to grasp it and exhibit twice that skill on the field of play to the admiration of all and sundry."– 'Super' Sam Suppey, June 2019

Polo with his Al Wasl Club colleagues, UAE

Polo displaying the SWAG cup as Ghana's best footballer in 1974

Chapter 10

FINALE

Aside winning the League and FA cups with Accra Hearts of Oak five times, Ahmed Polo also won the League Championship with Al Wasl in UAE four times between 1978 and 1983 while being voted the Best Professional player in that country. He has accumulated other prizes and chalked sterling achievements during his over 20 years on the turf. These include the following:

Year(s) of Award	Title	Awarding Institution
1974	Footballer of the Year	Sports Writers Association of Ghana, Ghana
1978	Gold, Africa Cup of Nations Cup (won with the Black Stars)	Confederation of African Football
1977-1978	3rd and 4th best African Player	Confederation of African Football
1984	Won tournament with Qatar FC	Doha, Qatar
1987	Dedication and Valour	Sports Writers Association of Ghana
2006	Grand Medalist	Ghana National Highest Award of Excellence, Government of Ghana
2006	Breaking Down Barriers (using soccer as a tool for peace building to make the world a better place)	FIFA/Coca Cola Award
2011	Soccer Dribbling Legend Award	Ghanaian Citizens in America (alongside Rev. Osei Kofi and Alhaji Ibrahim Sunday)

What more can one do beyond stockpiling such an array of medals within one's lifetime playing soccer with a nagging groin injury?

*"The Dribbling Magician was in a class of his own. Any football fan who did not have the opportunity of ever watching Ahmed Polo in the 1970s and 80s has really missed eye-catching, jaw-dropping and awe-inspiring football. Watching him, one could neither sit nor stand because he always had something special to spice up the game. When Lawal, Hearts of Oak's treasured left-winger, left for Kotoko in the early 1970s, Hearts fans wondered who could fill that gap. Miraculously, Polo appeared on the scene. As a teenager, we the fans were skeptical and indeed scared particularly at a time when we were then going to play Kotoko in Kumasi featuring their dreaded right full back Dan 'Iddi Amin' Oppong. Polo not only distinguished himself in that match to allay our fears by making light-work of the much-feared Dan Oppong, he also announced to the rest of Ghana that a new football sensation had arrived and was going to dominate the scene for years. I have never, ever in all my life, ever set eyes on a finer footballer. He took the game to a level that has never been attained by any other. Polo is simply the greatest!" – **Maxwell Koranteng, Hearts of Oak National Chapters' Committee Chair/Organiser, August 2019**

"Polo was easily the dribbler's dribbler and the wonder kid of his generation. Barely 16 when he began to lace his boots with Accra Hearts of Oak in the top flight of Ghana football, Ahmed Polo was an instant hit. Doubtless, he was a star incarnate in the early 1970s as he led a fearsome frontline of comparatively older teammates to tear apart opposing defenses. You could not mention Polo without the combined team of marauding mates that fondly came to be known as the 'Fearsome Fivesome'… Such was the influence of the young dribbling ace that not even the then 'Iddi Amin' of Ghanaian defenders Dan Oppong of Kumasi Asante Kotoko fame could withstand the wizardry of the Nima-born prodigy." **– Felix Abayateye, former Sports Editor, Ghanaian Times, September 2019**

Additional Gallery

The Wonder Boy

Celebration time: *Colleagues Anas Seidu, Michelle Lomo, Robert Hammond and Sam Ampeh join Polo to blow candles on his birthday cake while in Black Stars camp some time in 1975. They had been visited by then Hearts' Team Manager G. W. Amarteifio and a staunch supporter and business tycoon from Takoradi, Mr. Tonffick, admirers of The Dribbling Magician.*

Chapter 11

UP-CLOSE WITH THE FOOTBALL PROFESSOR

Q: When were you born and where do you come from?

11th November 1955 at Nima 441, but my people come from Chamba in the Northern Region but originally from the Kusuntu people of Togo; my ancestors have lived in Ghana for decades.

Q: Who were your parents?

Alhaji Ahmed Abdul Rahman and Hajia Hawa Abdul Rahman (both of blessed memory).

Q: Where did you live and grow up and who are some of your childhood colleagues?

Around Nima with Anas Seidu, Ibrahim Labaran and Ahmed Yakubu my senior brother.

Q: Tell us about your family, please.
Family of origin: we were 5 in all – 4 males and 1 female.
Family of procreation: I have 3 wives and 8 children in all, 5 boys and 3 girls.

Q: Did any of your kids take after you?
All my boys play football, but none has displayed the kind of skills to my standard or expectation even though I am trying to help them to improve.

Q: In which year did you start playing for Hearts of Oak?
In 1972 in a match against Susubribi.

Q: When did you get or sustain the injury that nearly truncated your football career?

It was in 1976. I have had to receive treatment from local herbal treatment sources, the 37 Military Hospital, Korle Bu Teaching Hospital and even from abroad (the Czech Republic and Germany).

Q: In which year did you start playing for the Black Stars of Ghana?
In 1973 in a match against Zaire (now Democratic Republic of Congo).

Q: What are you hobbies?
Watching polo, watching soccer and boxing.

Q: The "Best Signposts" in your football career:

- **Best goalkeepers you encountered/admired:**

  Goalkeepers Owusu Mensah, Sannie Abdulai, Henry Lante France (Duru) and Joe Carr (Agyinamoa).

- **Best defenders:**

  Kuuku Dadzie (Cool Max), Isaac Acquaye (Disco Face), Offei Ansah and P.S.K. Paha.

- **Best schemers/mid-fielders:**

  'Bomber' Mama Musa (Acquah), 'Golden Boy' Abdul Razak, Adolf Armah and Abedi Ayew 'Pele'.

- **Best attackers:**

  Dan Owusu, 'Goal Thief' Peter Lamptey, Opoku Afriyie 'Bayie' and George 'Jair' Alhassan.

- **Best coaches you worked under as a player:**

  Coaches Adabie, Osam Doudu, Afranie and Ben Koufie.

- **Best players you have coached and mentored:**

  Abedi Ayew, Stephen 'Tornado' Appiah, Shafiu Abdul Fatau and Shamo Quaye.

- **Best three matches you really enjoyed of all-time:**

  1. Black Stars vrs Morocco (World Cup Qualifying Match in Kumasi, 1975, 2-0)

  2. Hearts vrs AKOTEX (FA Cup finals, Accra Sports Stadium, 1977, 2-2)

  3. Hearts vrs Mufuliara Wanderers of Zambia, (Africa Clubs Championship Cup Semi-Finals, 'Miracle of El Wak', 1977, 3-0)

- Worst/regrettable matches played:

  Hearts vrs US Goiree of Senegal, 2nd leg, 1985 in Accra. I was very sick before the match and requested not to be fielded but was forced to play. I wept when putting on the jersey in the dressing room because I simply did not have the strength to play. What made it more painful was that some high-profile persons and colleagues thought I was just feigning injury. I spent less than 3 minutes on the field without kicking a ball and got replaced eventually.

  It was also a pity that I could not feature in the finals of the club championship cup that year in the two-leg matches against Hafia Club of Guinea. If I had, perhaps Hearts could have won the cup as far back as 1977.

Q: Do you have any regrets in your life?

None, immensely thankful to God for His manifold blessings.

Q: Any advice to the current crop of players?

They need to heed to wise counsel. They have opportunities now more than we used to have in our time. They should make good use of what they earn and overall they should be God-fearing because one day, we shall be accountable to God for our lives.

Q: How do you see the future of Ghana football?

Bright, but we have to know and appreciate our identity and brand of football; we need:

a) clear vision,

b) good technical direction,

c) sharp methodology and sound philosophy to move our football forward e.g. the five-year development plan which I have outlined and intend to operationalize BUT for the COVID-19 pandemic. Even others can take and run with it if I am unable to implement it later. The plan is aimed at winning the World Cup one day, our ultimate objective. It is not impossible to achieve!

Q: How should we organize our football administration to produce/achieve better results?

a) Development of coaches with sound technical direction via practical sessions through the regions similar to the 'samba' football of Brazil and a return to our brand of football ('agror' – good passing game of Ghana);

b) Development of youth football through academies and the like;

c) Take them through age group processes (Under-15, Under-17, Under-23 etc. thereby grooming them to play together to develop the synergies to make them gel well).

In our time, because of the way we developed our home-grown talents, short and small players like Opoku Afriyie and Dan Owusu could outjump and outwit taller and stronger players to score goals and beat teams with physically bigger opponents.

Q: How is your football academy doing?

In spite of challenges here and there, we are not doing badly at all and operating at about 80% of our capacity or potential.

At the end of Polo's professional soccer career in UAE, the sports authorities could not help but shower him with gifts galore — citation, trophy, medals etc. They found him a rare gem of a footballer!

Polo with team mates of Hearts of Oak in 1985 with the likes of Joe Odoi, Joe Amoateng, Sampson Lamptey, Offei Ansah, Adolf Armah, Opoku Afriyie and others

The Professor being carried shoulder-high by fans after helping to win a match with Hearts. Many of such scenes characterised his matches because he was very instrumental in many of Hearts victories together with winning Man-of-the-Match awards

The 'Superamus' leading his charges in an international match (George Lamptey, Sam Yeboah, Joe Amoateng and co.)

As Hearts of Oak skipper, Polo is seen here exchanging pennants before a match with the captain of Jaraaf F/C of Senegal
(Clubs Championship match)

Though young, Polo's high sense of responsibility and dedication catapulted him to the captainship of Hearts in his early 20s even with much older players around

"It is my pleasure, Sir", Polo seems to be saying as he was being introduced to the then Head of State Gen. Kutu Acheampong who was a big fan of the Dribbling Ace by Black Stars Captain Kwasi Owusu

In the company of Black Stars team mates in the mid-1970s (Kwasi Owusu, Kuuku Dadzie, Skipper Awuley Quaye, Mama Acquah, Joe Sam, Goalkeeper Joe Carr, Anas Seidu among others)

With Hearts of Oak team mates in the mid-1970s – Goalkeeper Henry Lante France (Duru), My Son Sam Amarteifio, Afro Joe Dakota, Tetteh Chandu, Mama Musa (Acquah), "Moshe Dayan" Boye Otinkorang, Aryee Acquah, 'Slow Motion' Joe Ghartey, 'Gabo' Christian Madus and others

Polo with Hearts of Oak team of the early 1970s – 'Speedster' Kofi Bruce, Addo Quarcoo, Goalkeeper 'Super' Sam Suppey, 'Seaman' Tony Micah, Addoquaye Addo, Robert Folley, Ofei Ansah and co.

Family Life

Abibatu Bade Kuma Polo, Polo's wife

Farida Ali Mohammed Polo, wife

Gloria Tsipoto, Polo's Wife (from Gabon)

Children of Madam Abibatu Bade Kuma

Children of Madam Farida Ali Mohammed

Daughter of Madam Gloria Tsipoto

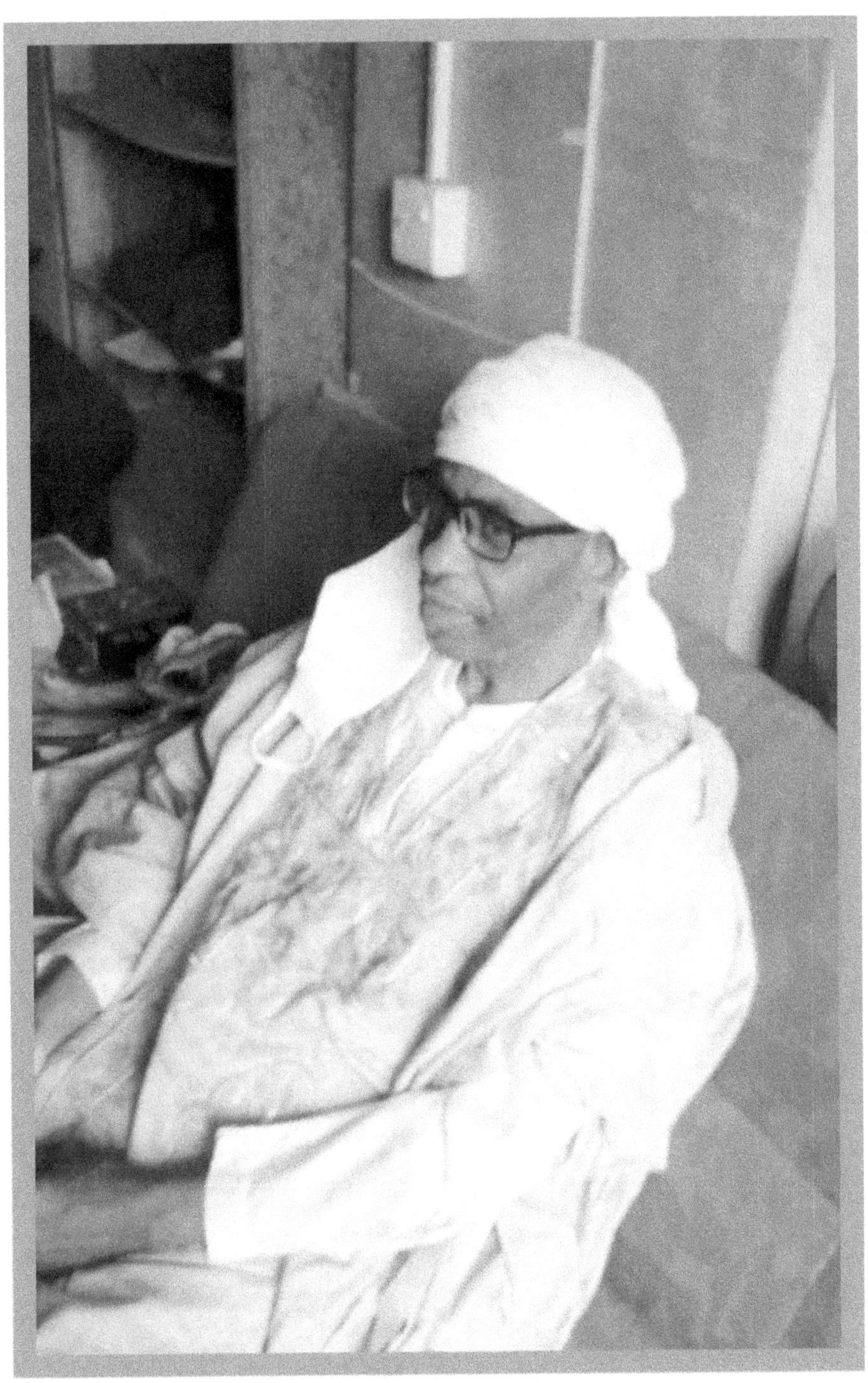

Polo as he looks like today